HMS PINAFORE

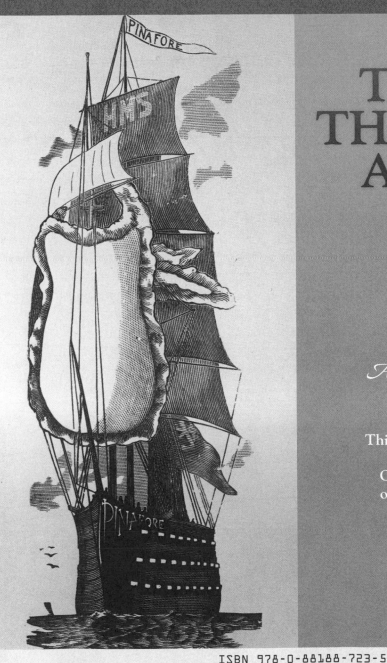

or
THE LASS THAT LOVED A SAILOR

Book by
W.S. Gilbert

Music by
Arthur Sullivan

Authentic Version Edited by
Bryceson Treharne

This score includes all the dialogue.

Orchestral material is available
on rental from G. Schirmer, Inc.

P.O. Box 572
445 Bellvale Road
Chester, NY 10918
(845) 469-2271
(845) 469-7544 (fax)
www.schirmer.com

Ed. 1623

ISBN 978-0-88188-723-5

G. SCHIRMER, Inc.

DISTRIBUTED BY
HAL•LEONARD®
CORPORATION
7777 W. BLUEMOUND RD. P.O. BOX 13819 MILWAUKEE, WI 53213

T0057174

DRAMATIS PERSONAE

The Rt. Hon. Sir Joseph Porter, K.C.B ....First Lord of the Admiralty

Captain Corcoran ....Commander of *HMS Pinafore*

Ralph Rackstraw ....Able Seaman

Dick Deadeye ....Able Seaman

Bill Bobstay...Boatswain's Mate

Bob Becket ....Carpenter's Mate

Josephine ....The Captain's Daughter

Cousin Hebe ....Sir Joseph's First Cousin

Little Buttercup ....A Portsmouth Bumboat Woman

First Lord's Sisters, his Cousins, his Aunts, Sailors, Marines, etc.

Scene: Quarterdeck of *HMS Pinafore*, off Portsmouth

ACT I—Noon

ACT II—Night

MUSICAL NUMBERS

ARGUMENT

Some time before Act I opens, Ralph has fallen in love with Josephine, the daughter of his commanding officer, Captain Corcoran. Likewise, Little Buttercup, a buxom peddler-woman, has fallen in love with the Captain himself. Class pride, however, stands in the way of the natural inclinations of both the Corcorans to reciprocate Ralph's and Buttercup's affections. The Captain has, in fact, been arranging a marriage between his daughter and Sir Joseph Porter, First Lord of the Admiralty, who is of the social class above even the Corcorans.

When Act I opens, the sailors are merrily preparing the ship for Sir Joseph's inspection. The generally happy atmosphere on deck is marred only by Little Buttercup's hints of a dark secret she is hiding, by the misanthropic grumbling of Dick Deadeye, and by the love-lorn plaints of Ralph and Josephine. Sir Joseph appears, attended by a train of ladies (his relatives, who always follow him wherever he goes). He explains how he became Lord of the Admiralty and examines the crew, patronizingly encouraging them to feel that they are everyone's equal, except his. Like the Captain, he is very punctilious, demanding polite diction among the sailors at all times.

Josephine finds him insufferable. When Ralph again pleads his suit and finally threatens suicide, she agrees to elope. The act ends with the general rejoicing of the sailors at Ralph's success; only Dick Deadeye croaks his warning that their hopes will be frustrated.

Act II opens with the Captain in despair at the demoralization of his crew and the coldness of his daughter towards Sir Joseph. Little Buttercup tries to comfort him, and prophesies a change in store. But Sir Joseph soon appears and tells the Captain that Josephine has thoroughly discouraged him in his suit; he wishes to call the match off. The Captain suggests that perhaps his daughter feels herself inferior in social rank to Sir Joseph, and urges him to assure her that inequality of social rank should not be considered a barrier to marriage. This Sir Joseph does, not realizing that his words are as applicable to Josephine in relation to Ralph as they are to himself in relation to Josephine. He thinks that she accepts him, whereas actually she is reaffirming her acceptance of Ralph. They all join in a happy song.

Meanwhile, Dick Deadeye has made his way to the Captain, and informs him of the planned elopement of his daughter with Ralph. The Captain thereupon intercepts the elopers and, when he learns that Josephine was actually running away to marry Ralph, he is so incensed that he cries, "Damne!" Unfortunately, Sir Joseph and his relatives hear him and are horrified at his swearing; Sir Joseph sends him to his cabin in disgrace. But when Sir Joseph also learns from Ralph that Josephine was eloping, he angrily orders Ralph put in irons.

Little Buttercup now comes out with her secret, which solves the whole difficulty: she confesses that many years ago she had charge of nursing and bringing up Ralph and the Captain when they were babies. Inadvertantly, she got them mixed up; so the one who now was Ralph really should be the Captain, and the one now the Captain should be Ralph. This error is immediately rectified. The sudden reversal in the social status of Ralph and the Corcorans removes Sir Joseph as a suitor for Josephine's hand and permits her to marry Ralph, and her father to marry Buttercup. Sir Joseph resigns himself to marrying his cousin, Hebe.

GILBERT & SULLIVAN

W.S. Gilbert

Arthur Sullivan

THE GILBERT & SULLIVAN PARTNERSHIP
By Marie Eggold

In fourteen operettas over the course of twenty-five years, W.S. Gilbert and Arthur Sullivan etched their names in the history books forever. Their works not only created an English school of light opera, they whetted an appetite for musical theater in the United States and around the world. Their works have inspired a steady stream of recordings, revivals, books, and articles over the past century, with films and web sites appearing more recently. Gilbert and Sullivan have remained at the heart of the operetta repertoire for more than 100 years. Yet for Gilbert, who aspired to write serious dramas, and Sullivan, who aspired to write serious music, writing entertainment for the Victorian middle class was not quite fulfilling.

Although one seldom hears the names Gilbert and Sullivan spoken separately, the two had careers independent of one another. They were also remarkably different men. Gilbert was well over six feet tall and fair complected, with a rather grim face. Sullivan on the other hand was quite short, dark haired, and was known for an easy smile and twinkling eyes. As Gilbert aged, he retained a youthful vigor that allowed him to show off occasional dance steps in his later years, just to prove that he still could. Sullivan's health was poor. He was stricken with a painful kidney ailment and walked with a cane while still a young man. Gilbert was regarded as one of the most prominent dramatists of his day, while Sullivan was seen as someone with a tremendous gift that he failed to develop fully.

William Schwenck Gilbert

William Schwenck Gilbert was born on November 18, 1836, just a few months before the reign of Queen Victoria began. His father, Dr. William Gilbert, had served as a naval surgeon until an inheritance allowed him to retire to travel and write. In later years the younger Gilbert, called Schwenck by his family, would illustrate some of his father's publications. Schwenck studied law and practiced briefly, but soon turned his attention to writing. He was a frequent contributor to *Fun* magazine, publishing drawings, short stories, and dramatic criticism. Best remembered of his work from this time are the *Bab Ballads*, stories in verse that he signed with his childhood nickname. The name is short for "Babby," his family's twist on baby.

Topics and ideas from the *Bab Ballads* and other early works show up, fleshed out, in the operettas, as do several recurring themes. The Gilbert family often told the story of how Schwenck had been kidnapped while they were in Italy. He was only missing for a few hours, quickly returned for a small bit of money. But he claimed to have a memory of the event, likely just familiarity from hearing the tale repeated throughout his childhood. The idea of two children switched at birth, and the ensuing crisis of identity and social class, pops up again and again in his works, most notably in *The Pirates of Penzance*. Another theme was one of topsy-turvy worlds. Gilbert was fascinated by plots and scenarios based on things being just the opposite of what they should be. Virtue was evil, peace was war, etc. He explored the idea in his one-act extravaganza,

Topsyturveydom, which opened on March 21, 1874, returning to it throughout his career. By the mid-1870s, Gilbert was well-known as a playwright.

From the first "official" biography of Gilbert, which appeared in 1923, to the 1935 Hesketh Pearson book *Gilbert and Sullivan*, and his 1957 *Gilbert—His Life and Strife*, William Schwenck Gilbert was painted as a kindly, fairly typical British gentleman. In fact, Gilbert was a very difficult man. "I am an ill-tempered pig," he once wrote, "and I glory in it." In the book *Between Ourselves* (1930), Seymour Hicks wrote of Gilbert, "He always gave me the impression that he got up in the morning to see with whom he could have a quarrel." Indeed, Gilbert seemed to relish quarrels. He was an extremely litigious man. He saw personal slights at every turn and was not content until things were put right, in his favor of course. His stock line in such situations was, "I shall place the matter at once in the hands of my solicitor."

Arthur Sullivan

Arthur Sullivan, on the other hand, was a kind, likeable man with no great ego. He enjoyed having fun and was somewhat notorious for his various appetites, which included incessant travel, encounters with prostitutes, and constant indulging in fine foods and wines. He was born on May 13, 1842, to a bandmaster who filled his son's life with music and recognized the boy's talents early. By 1856, Arthur was a scholarship student at the Royal Academy of Music, studying at the Leipzig Conservatory from 1858 to 1861. His instructors there believed he had a greater musical gift than Brahms. Later it was said that he had greater ability than any English musician since Purcell. In the face of such lavish praise, his work in operettas, no matter how popular and successful they might be, was viewed by critics as a waste of a tremendous talent.

A conductor, educator, and organist, in addition to being a composer, Sullivan had written a good deal of "serious" music by the time he began his partnership with Gilbert. He always viewed his theater work as secondary to serious composition, which included choral works, a symphony, a ballet, and numerous hymns, the most famous being "Onward Christian Soldiers." Yet an article that appeared in the *Pall Mall Gazette* at the time of the premiere of *The Gondoliers* declared Sullivan England's most popular composer—popularity won by operettas. The same biographers who overlooked Gilbert's irascible nature treated Sullivan's easy-going personality and voracious appetites harshly.

The recipient of several honorary doctorates, Sullivan was not an intellectual, nor was he a literary man. He was, however, remembered by colleagues as a remarkable wit. Perhaps his greatest musical gift was his uncanny ability to contrive music to fit any lyric, any scene, and any mood. His music became an integral part of the theatrical scene, not a separate element. He would tailor his melodies to Gilbert's pattering poetry, gild a tune to match the sets or dances of a particular scene, and orchestrate the entire thing with grace and good humor.

The Partnership

The Gilbert and Sullivan partnership was actually a trio. The third partner was Richard D'Oyly Carte, who served as the catalyst who made the creative pair household names. Carte was the son of Richard Carte, a flautist and partner in the musical instrument manufacturing firm of Rudall, Carte and Co. He started out in his father's business, wrote some operettas, and conducted as well. But by the time he was twenty-five, he had set up his own theatrical and concert agency. Carte was not involved in Gilbert and Sullivan's first collaboration, *Thespis, or The Gods Grown Old*, which opened at the Gaiety Theatre on December 26, 1871. The libretto and score were never published and all but two numbers have been lost. Carte brought the writers together for *Trial By Jury*, which opened at the Royalty Theatre on March 25, 1875, performed with two other pieces. It outlived the productions with which it shared a bill and set Carte in motion. He interested several investing partners, leased the Opera Comique and announced the creation of the Comedy Opera Company. The company produced *The Sorcerer*, which opened on October 17, 1877, and *HMS Pinafore*, which opened on May 25, 1878. Although *Pinafore* had opened to receptive audiences and positive reviews, an unusually hot summer kept people out of the theaters and began a rift between Carte and the investors that eventually led to their separation. This left Carte free to form a partnership with the librettist and composer. The company was first known as Mr. D'Oyly Carte's Company until the name was changed in 1889 to The D'Oyly Carte Opera Company. With Carte at the helm, Gilbert and Sullivan created *The Pirates of Penzance*, which opened in England on December 30, 1879 and in New York a day later. *Patience* followed, opening in London on April 23, 1881.

Carte then built the Savoy Theatre in London, devoted to the production of the work of Gilbert and Sullivan. Erected on the site of the palace of Savoy that had been destroyed in the late 1300s, it was a strikingly modern theater. In fact, it was the world's first theater to be completely lit by electricity. With electricity came the ability to create lighting effects, which helped draw audiences to productions. A generator located in an empty lot beside the theater provided the power. A few years later Carte opened the Savoy Hotel on that lot, which was also a progressive building at the time. The Savoy Theatre hosted the premieres of *Iolanthe* in 1882, *Princess Ida* in 1884, *The Mikado* in 1885, *Ruddigore* in 1887, *The Yeoman of the Guard* in 1888, *The Gondoliers* in 1889, *Utopia Limited* in 1893, and *The Grand Duke* in 1896.

The Ocean Was Not Always Blue

Despite the levity of the operettas, the partnership was not bliss. Carte was building a new theater, the Royal English Opera House, in which he intended to premiere Sullivan's grand opera, *Ivanhoe*. Although the January 31, 1891 premiere was received with accolades, the public was not ready to embrace grand opera as it had embraced light opera. Carte eventually sold the theater. Meanwhile, as *Ruddigore* was running and Sullivan was preparing *Ivanhoe*, Gilbert took a close look at the accounts for the partnership. He found an expense of £140 to re-carpet the Savoy lobby and took offense. He felt that he and Sullivan should not be charged for such an extravagance. Sullivan sided with Carte. What ensued, remembered as the famous "Carpet Quarrel," created a wound that would not heal. The partnership was dissolved. Eventually the trio put their differences aside and created *Utopia Limited* and *The Grand Duke*, but things were never the same. Even in the best of times, Gilbert and Sullivan referred to each other by their surnames. Gilbert was constantly at war with one or another cast member, making rehearsals awkward affairs by giving his undivided attention to everyone but the party at whom he was angry. When the offending actor did a scene, Gilbert would pointedly ignore the goings-on, turning his back to the stage and making a great show of talking to someone until the scene was over.

Following *The Gondoliers*, the Savoy was largely devoted to revivals of Gilbert and Sullivan's operettas, or to pieces written by Sullivan with another librettist. But the partnership Gilbert/Sullivan/D'Oyly Carte would not have survived the 1890s regardless of the "Carpet Quarrel." Both Sullivan and Carte were in failing health. Sullivan's health had been in a long decline, his kidney disease causing him horrendous pain. He died on November 22, 1900. Carte survived him by just six months. Gilbert however, maintained a vigorous lifestyle to the end. On May 29, 1911 the seventy-four-year-old Gilbert endeavored to teach two women to swim in the lake he had created at his home. When one of the women floundered, Gilbert dove in to save her, suffering a fatal heart attack in the water.

The Legacy

The magic of the Gilbert and Sullivan partnership lay in the cutting wit and perfectionism of Gilbert, who micro-managed details of rehearsals, and his ability to craft a plot of many convoluted layers, only to have it all sort out neatly in the end. Along the way he would poke fun at social conventions, the law, and romance. Sullivan was the one who made froth of this wit. He could craft melodies that instantly projected the dramatic intent of Gilbert's lines. He was fearless in his treatment of rhythms. He rose to such challenges as setting the mouthfuls of lyrics presented by "I am the Very Model of a Modern Major General," creating an operetta classic. Their contributions did not go unrecognized. Sullivan was knighted in 1883. Gilbert was knighted in 1907.

The D'Oyly Carte Opera Company continued presenting and touring the works of Gilbert and Sullivan until financial difficulties forced it to close in 1982. The D'Oyly Carte Opera Trust had been formed in 1961, when the copyrights ran out on the operettas. In her will, Dame Bridget Carte left £1 million to the trust, earmarking it to reform the company. The company reappeared in 1988, returning to the Savoy Theatre in 2000.

HMS PINAFORE
By Marie Eggold

HMS Pinafore, or the Lass that Loved a Sailor, was the fourth collaboration of W.S. Gilbert and Arthur Sullivan. It was almost their last. Despite glowing reviews following its opening at the Opera Comique in London, the "entirely nautical comic opera in two acts" almost floundered within weeks. Had it actually failed, it would likely have meant the end of the creative partnership that redefined theater in Victorian England and set the stage for what we now know as modern musical theater. As it was, *Pinafore* found its audience and was followed quickly by *The Pirates of Penzance*. The rest, as they say, is history.

HMS Pinafore began with Gilbert, long before he knew anything of Arthur Sullivan. The roots of the operetta can be found in several of Gilbert's earlier works, including several of his *Bab Ballads*. One of these told the story of Captain Reece of the ship the *Mantelpiece*. Elements of the story were also drawn from *The Baby's Vengeance*, a ballad about infant swapping that had its roots in Gilbert's brief childhood kidnapping episode. In *The Bumboat Woman* we first meet Buttercup under the name Pineapple Poll. The story also bears some resemblance to *Dr. Middy*, one of the children's books written by Gilbert's father. The *Pinafore* plot is also quite similar to that of *The Sorcerer*, the previous Gilbert & Sullivan creation.

From these various elements Gilbert began to fashion a new libretto early in 1878. As was his custom, he began with a scenario and progressed to song lyrics. He turned to writing the dialogue once the songs were well underway, in early May. If Sullivan found a particular passage of lyrics troubling or difficult to set to music, Gilbert would rework them. Sections of the show were rewritten after rehearsals had already begun. Always the perfectionist, Gilbert decided early on that the sets for *Pinafore* had to be absolutely authentic. On April 13, 1878, both Gilbert and Sullivan traveled to Portsmouth, where a number of Navy vessels lay in anchor. They were taken aboard several of the ships, including the HMS *Thunderer* and Admiral Nelson's old flagship the HMS *Victory*. Gilbert did careful, detailed sketches of sailors' uniforms and details of the ships structure and equipment. Gilbert insisted on accuracy down to the knots on the rigging. He intended to create a British man-of-war on the stage. During rehearsals of *Pinafore*, one of the actors pulled one of the ropes on the set out of place and took bets as to whether Gilbert would notice and if so, when. The librettist/director spotted it before the rehearsal even began. Costumes too had to be absolutely accurate. To that end, Gilbert ordered the sailors' uniforms from a tailor in Portsmouth who supplied the British navy. When Gilbert was done with his tour onboard the Navy ships, he headed home to an exact model of the Opera Comique stage, built at one-half inch scale. Here he designed the set and mapped out the movements of each character. Three-inch tall wooden blocks indicated male cast members. Women were represented by two-and-one-half inch tall blocks. By the time he walked into the first rehearsal, every entrance and exit of each actor had been meticulously plotted, as had all staging, down to the smallest movements. The chorus of sailors in the production were drilled explicitly in how to man the fictional ship.

While Gilbert was creating his realistic set and crew, Sullivan was struggling with composition. Although the music for this operetta is considered among his finest, he was writing in the throes of a terrible attack of the kidney disease that would plague him for the rest of his life. He later described working on a few bars of music at a time, between waves of debilitating pain. Gilbert was not entirely well at this point either, dogged by bouts of migraine and gout. It was Sullivan who came up with the show's title sometime during the writing.

Pinafore opened at the Opera Comique on May 25, 1878. Final rehearsals had run until 3:30 a.m. that morning. Gilbert paced the streets during the first performance, peeking into the theater just a few times. The critics, for the most part, smiled on the show. They loved the "chorus that acts" and the realistic sets and costumes. The weather, however, was not so kind. London was having one the hottest springs in its history. The Opera Comique, a stuffy, stifling place on a good day, was terribly uncomfortable in the heat. Gilbert and Sullivan were not yet the household names they would become; their names on a show did not yet guarantee a hit. In addition, many well-to-do Victorian Londoners still had serious reservations about attending the theater. It was not considered appropriate entertainment for those of a certain social station, an attitude the Gilbert and Sullivan successes helped to change.

Within days of the opening, due to the heat, *Pinafore's* tickets sales began to fall off. Richard D'Oyly Carte found himself in the position of reassuring his co-directors/backers, who were ready to close the show. Notices of the closing went up, were taken down, and went up again. The actors agreed to take a pay cut of one third to keep the production running. The orchestra was pared down and a new group of musicians was hired, willing to play for less money than the original players. Sullivan, who had been traveling, returned to hear the bargain orchestra and threatened to withdraw his music if better players were not found immediately. The heat persisted into June and July, and people stayed away in droves. In the end it was Sullivan who steered the *HMS Pinafore* back on course. He was conducting a series of Promenade Concerts (The Proms) at Covent Garden. On one of these July concerts he included an selection of melodies from *Pinafore* that had been arranged for orchestra by Hamilton Clarke. People loved the music, and the piece had to be repeated three times the first night it was played. Suddenly, the entire audience wanted to see the show. The box office soon turned around and *Pinafore* started making money. By fall the show was doing splendidly in London. Lines from the libretto were becoming trendy catch phrases throughout the city.

On November 25, 1878, an unofficial production of *Pinafore* opened in Boston. *Pinafore* mania hit the States almost immediately. Productions of *Pinafore* ran at six different theaters at once in Philadelphia. From church choirs to puppet theater, *Pinafore* was turning up everywhere. But royalties were not turning up in the pockets of the show's creators. There were no international copyright laws at the time, so Gilbert and Sullivan saw no money from these American productions. Perhaps more galling, at least to perfectionist Gilbert, these were productions only loosely based on the original. There was no published score, so musical sources were highly suspect. Gilbert's detailed sets and costumes were nowhere to be found on American stages. Some productions were blatant, slapstick parodies of the original, with such names as *His Mud Scow Pinafore, H,M,S, Needlefore, or the Lass that Loved a Tailor.*

Carte knew that something had to be done about the American piracy of *Pinafore*. But he also knew that something had to be done about the meddling and interfering of the co-directors/backers that he had brought together to form the Comedy Opera Company. He decided that when the lease on the Opera Comique came up for renewal on July 31, 1879, he would renew it in his own name and set off without the other backers. In the long run this meant the dissolution of the Comedy Opera Company and the creation of the now famous partnership between Carte and Gilbert and Sullivan, the D'Oyly Carte Opera Company. In the short run, however, it meant high drama at the operetta.

Carte set up the new partnership and lease agreement, buying out his previous partners. He appointed Michael Gunn to run things, granting him power of attorney over the affairs of the theater company. Carte then sailed for the States at the end of June to see what could be done about the piracy of *Pinafore* in the colonies. Now that *Pinafore* was doing well in London, after the slow first months, Carte's partners had no great desire to be relieved of their share of the production. They immediately fired Gunn and announced that Carte was no longer running the company. Gunn went to court and won his position back, but the former partners were not happy. On July 31 they arrived at the theater with a gang of men. Several large vans were waiting outside. They burst into the theater in mid-performance and began grabbing set pieces and props, attempting to load them into the vans. The backers insisted that they were the rightful owners of these goods. The stories told about that night vary somewhat in details. What is certain is that the audience got more of a show than they paid for. Some audience members, hearing the crashing commotion coming from backstage, feared a fire had broken out and quickly left the theater. Some accounts have Buttercup valiantly carrying on with her song while the fracas backstage all but drowned her out. Eventually, the performance was stopped and one of the actors came forward and explained the situation in a curtain speech. Meanwhile, stagehands and chorus men were waging a pitched battle behind the curtain. The tide turned, thanks in part to Gilbert's insistence on accuracy in costumes; he had equipped many of the chorus men with actual bayonets.

The battle may have been won but the war was far from over. Richard Barker, who had been seriously injured in the backstage melee, brought suit against Carte's former partners. The partners, for their part, felt they owned the rights to the show and mounted their own production within shouting distance of the Opera Comique. Gilbert immediately posted notices stating that the Opera Comique was the only authorized production. The other production failed in short order. A lengthy court battle ended in favor of Carte, Gilbert, and Sullivan.

Carte, in the States by now, had other things to worry about. He found eight theaters in New York, in the space of five blocks, all running pirate productions of *Pinafore*. Plans were made for Gilbert, Sullivan, and a company of actors to sail for America. They would mount an official *Pinafore* in New York and there prepare to unveil their newest creation, *The Pirates of Penzance*, before theatrical pirates could possibly get any sources for productions. When Gilbert, Sullivan, and the British actors sailed into New York harbor, they were greeted by a flotilla of ships carrying various pirate casts of *Pinafore*, all singing and playing music from the show. One dissenting tug boat bore a "No Pinafore" banner and blew its whistle repeatedly to drown out the cacophonous musical tributes.

The officially sanctioned *Pinafore* opened in New York at the Fifth Avenue Theatre on December 1, 1879. Some accounts place Gilbert on-stage in costume, keeping a close watch on his cast of British principals and American chorus members. *Pirates* would open in New York soon after, on December 31, 1879. While Carte, Gilbert and Sullivan were in the US, a matinee production of *Pinafore*, featuring child actors, began running at the Opera Comique in London. When Gilbert returned to England and saw the production, he was so pleased that he immediately ran out and purchased boxes of candy for the young performers. He later made a children's story of *Pinafore*.

With the *Pinafore* libretto, Gilbert took liberal pot-shots at the class system of British society as well as at the Royal Navy. The part of the Sir Joseph bore a striking resemblance to W.H. Smith, Britain's actual First Lord of the Admiralty. Smith had been appointed to the post because of his exceptional organizational and administrative skills. He did not, however, have any knowledge of sailing nor of the navy. Not long after *Pinafore's* popularity soared, even Benjamin Disraeli, who as Prime Minister had appointed Smith, was referring to him as "Pinafore Smith." Gilbert's topsy-turvy reversal of social stations poked fun at the social order of Britain as well. Audiences loved the humor and music. While navy-men took exception to the comic portrayal of First Lord of the Admiralty, they admired Gilbert's realistic depiction of a man-of-war. The show has never lost its popularity, remaining one of the three most often performed of the Gilbert and Sullivan comic operas.

HMS PINAFORE
Selected Discography

Recommended recordings:

1. The 1922 D'Oyly Carte recording, conducted by Harry Norris and G.W. Byng, recorded in London between May 31, 1922 and March 15, 1923, released in on 78 rpm by HMV in 1924 and Victor in 1925, reissued on LP in 1978 by Pearl, on CD in 1998 by Sounds on CD, in 1999 by J.C. Lockwood 78s to CD, and on an Opera Classics compilation with other G&S works (this disc will play only on a computer). Sir Joseph Porter: Frederick Ranalow/Darrell Fancourt/Henry Millidge; Captain Corcoran: Sydney Granville; Ralph Rackstraw: James Hay/Walter Glynne; Dick Deadeye: Darrell Fancourt/Frederick Hobbs; Bill Bobstay: Sydney Granville; Bob Becket: Edward Halland; Josephine: Violet Essex/Bessie Jones; Little Buttercup: Bertha Lewis/Nellie Walker; Hebe: Pamela Baselow; D'Oyly Carte Opera Chorus.

2. The 1930 D'Oyly Carte recording, conducted by Malcolm Sargent, issued on 78rpm in 1930 by HMV and in 1931 by RCA Victor, on LP in 1952 by RCA Victor, on LP in 1955 by EMI/World HMV (Australia), on LP in 1969 by EMI, on LP in 1981 by Arabesque, on LP in 1982 on Arabesque, on CD in 1986 by Arabesque, in 1994 by Happy Days with *Mikado*, in 1996 by Romophone with *Pirates*, and in 2000 on 78s to CD. Sir Joseph Porter: Henry Lytton; Captain Corcoran: George Baker; Ralph Rackstraw: Charles Goulding; Dick Deadeye: Darrell Fancourt; Bill Bobstay: Sydney Granville; Bob Becket: Stuart Robertson; Josephine: Elsie Griffin; Little Buttercup: Bertha Lewis; Hebe: Nellie Briercliffe; D'Oyly Carte Opera Chorus; London Symphony Orchestra.

3. The 1949 D'Oyly Carte recording, conducted by Isidore Godfrey, released in 1949 on 78 rpm by Decca, on 78 and LP by London, on LP in 1950 by Decca, in 1980 by Decca Viva on cassette, on CD in 2000 by Sounds on CD, also on CD on Pearl in 2000, and on CD in 2001 by Naxos. Sir Joseph Porter: Martyn Green; Captain Corcoran: Leslie Rands; Ralph Rackstraw: Leonard Osborn; Dick Deadeye: Darrell Fancourt; Bill Bobstay: Richard Walker; Bob Becket: L. Radley Flynn; Josephine: Muriel Harding; Little Buttercup: Ella Halman; Hebe: Joan Gillingham; D'Oyly Carte Opera Chorus and Orchestra.

4. The 1958 Glyndebourne recording, conducted by Sir Malcolm Sargent, released on LP in 1958 and 1961 by HMV, in 1985 on digitally re-mastered LP by EMI/Angel, on LP and CD in 1989 by EMI with *Yeomen of the Guard*, on CD in 1992 by EMI with *Trial by Jury*, in 1998 by HMV with *Trial by Jury*, in 2001 by EMI as part of a 16-disc set of all nine of Sargent's Glyndebourne recordings. Sir Joseph Porter: George Baker; Captain Corcoran: John Cameron; Ralph Rackstraw: Richard Lewis; Dick Deadeye: Owen Brannigan; Bill Bobstay: James Milligan/John Cameron; Bob Becket: James Milligan/Owen Brannigan; Josephine: Elsie Morison; Little Buttercup: Monica Sinclair; Hebe: Marjorie Thomas; Glyndebourne Festival Chorus; Pro Arte Orchestra.

5. The highly recommended 1960 D'Oyly Carte recording, with complete dialogue, conducted by Isidore Godfrey, released on LP in 1960 by Decca and London, in the late 1960s by Decca with *Iolanthe* and *Pirates*, on LP in 1984 by Decca, on CD in 1989 by Decca/London. Sir Joseph Porter: John Reed; Captain Corcoran: Jeffery Skitch; Ralph Rackstraw: Thomas Round; Dick Deadeye: Donald Adams; Bill Bobstay: George Cook; Bob Becket: Eric Wilson-Hyde; Josephine: Jean Hindmarsh; Little Buttercup: Gillian Knight; Hebe: Joyce Wright; D'Oyly Carte Opera Chorus; New Symphony Orchestra of London.

6. The 1987 New Sadler's Wells Opera recording of a newly researched edition by David Russell Hulme, conducted by Simon Phipps, released on LP and CD in 1987 by MCA, on CD in 1987 on TER, in 1992 on Boots, in 1994 by Loch International, in 1995 by Showstoppers, in 1998 by Showtime, c. 1999 by Madacy, and in 1999 by Jay records. Sir Joseph Porter: Nicholas Grace; Captain Corcoran: Gordon Sandison; Ralph Rackstraw: Christopher Gillett; Dick Deadeye: Thomas Lawlor; Bill Bobstay: Paul Parfitt; Bob Becket: Paul Thomson; Josephine: Elizabeth Ritchie; Little Buttercup: Linda Ormiston; Hebe: Janine Roebuck; New Sadler's Wells Opera Chorus and Orchestra.

7. The 1994 Welsh National Opera recording, conducted by Sir George Mackerras, released on CD in 1994 by Telarc, reissued in 1999 with all of the Mackerras/Telarc recordings. Sir Joseph Porter: Richard Suart; Captain Corcoran: Thomas Allen; Ralph Rackstraw: Michael Schade; Dick Deadeye: Donald Adams; Bill Bobstay: Richard Van Allan; Bob Becket: John King (Trio No. 10)/Philip Lloyd Evans (Octet No. 19); Josephine: Rebecca Evans; Little Buttercup: Felicity Palmer; Hebe: Valerie Seymour; Welsh National Opera Chorus and Orchestra.

8. The New D'Oyly Carte Opera recording released in 2000, conducted by John Owen Edwards, released on CD in 2000 by TER. Sir Joseph Porter: Gordon Sandison; Captain Corcoran: Tom McVeigh; Ralph Rackstraw: Alfred Boe; Dick Deadeye: Simon Wilding; Bill Bobstay: Stephen Davis; Bob Becket: James Cleverton; Josephine: Yvonne Barclay; Little Buttercup: Frances McCafferty; Hebe: Gaynor Keeble; the New D'Oyly Carte Opera Chorus and Orchestra.

HMS PINAFORE
Selected Filmography and Videography

1. In the infancy of television NBC broadcast *Pinafore*, conducted by Harold Sanford; it aired on September 5, 1939. Since this predated the kinescope, there is no record of the performance.

2. The 1972 film by Gilbert and Sullivan for All, conducted by Peter Murray, video release by Musical Collectibles. Sir Joseph Porter: John Cartier; Captain Corcoran: Michael Wakeham; Ralph Rackstraw: Thomas Round; Dick Deadeye: Donald Adams; Bill Bobstay: Lawrence Richard; Bob Becket: John Banks; Josephine: Valerie Masterson; Little Buttercup: Helen Landis; Hebe: Vera Ryan; G&S Festival Chorus and Orchestra.

3. The 1973 film, made for television, of the D'Oyly Carte Opera Company production, conducted by Royston Nash, released on VHS c.1981 by Precision Video, in 1986 by Channel 5 Video, in 1993 by Polygram with the 1992 New D'Oyly Carte *Mikado*. Sir Joseph Porter: John Reed; Captain Corcoran: Michael Rayner; Ralph Rackstraw: Malcolm Williams; Dick Deadeye: John Ayldon; Bill Bobstay: Jon Ellison; Bob Becket: John Broad; Josephine: Pamela Field; Little Buttercup: Lyndsie Holland; Hebe: Pauline Wales; D'Oyly Carte Opera Chorus and Orchestra.

4. The 1981 Stratford Festival production, videotape, conducted by Berthold Carrière, directed by Leon Major, released on VHS in 1995 by the Stratford Festival. Sir Joseph Porter: Eric Donkin; Captain Corcoran: Michael Burgess; Ralph Rackstraw: James MacLean; Dick Deadeye: Avo Kittask; Bill Bobstay: Paul Massell; Bob Becket: Kenneth Baker; Josephine: Katherine Terrell; Little Buttercup: Patricia Kern; Hebe: Anne Linden.

5. The videotape of the 1982 Brent Walker production, conducted by Alexander Faris, released on VHS in 1982 by Brent Walker Productions, on videodisc in 1984 by Pioneer Artists, on VHS in 1986 by Woolworth, in 1991 by BraveWorld Video, in 1994 by Polygram Video, in 1996 by Opera World, and in 1999 by Roadshow (an Australian release that included *Cox and Box*, *Trial by Jury*, and *The Sorcerer*). Sir Joseph Porter: Frankie Howard; Captain Corcoran: Peter Marshall; Ralph Rackstraw: Michael Bulman; Dick Deadeye: Alan Watt; Bill Bobstay: Gordon Sandison; Josephine: Meryl Drower; Little Buttercup: Della Jones; Hebe: Anne Mason; the Ambrosian Opera Chorus and London Symphony Orchestra.

6. The 1997 Australian Essgee Entertainment production, conducted and re-orchestrated by Kevin Hocking, released on VHS in Australia and New Zealand 1997 by Essgee Entertainment, in 2001 with Essgee's *Pirates* and *Mikado*. Sir Joseph Porter: Drew Forsythe; Captain Corcoran: David Gould; Ralph Rackstraw: Simon Gallaher; Dick Deadeye: Jon English; Bill Bobstay: Jason Barry-Smith; Josephine: Helen Donaldson; Little Buttercup: Amanda Muggleton (*Australia*)/Rima Te Wiata (*New Zealand*); Sir Joseph's Sister, Cousin, & Aunt (The Absolutely Fabulettes): Marissa Craig, Andrea Gallaher, Melissa Langton.

GILBERT'S "BAB" ILLUSTRATIONS

W. S. Gilbert's nickname as a child was "Bab," the family's shortened form for baby. He illustrated each of his librettos with drawings, signed with "Bab." These are some of his illustrations for *HMS Pinafore*.

"But still I'm called Buttercup—poor Little Buttercup, sweet Little Buttercup I!" (Buttercup and Captain Corcoran)

"I copied all the letters in a hand so free, that now I am the Ruler of the Queen's Navee!" (Sir Joseph)

"Gaily tripping, lightly skipping" (Sir Joseph's relatives)

A stylized drawing of Josephine as a princess with a tiara.

"Kind Captain, I've important information" (Dick Deadeye)

H. M. S. Pinafore

or

The Lass That Loved A Sailor

W. S. GILBERT

ARTHUR SULLIVAN

Overture

2

Andante

col pedale

Allegro vivace

38261

3

4

Vivace

ACT I

No. 1 Introduction and Opening Chorus—(Sailors)
"We sail the ocean blue"

SCENE:— *Quarter-deck of H.M.S. Pinafore. Sailors, led by Boatswain, discovered cleaning brasswork, splicing rope, etc.*

Allegretto pesante

(Enter Buttercup, with large basket on her arm.

No. 2 Recitative and Aria— (Buttercup)
"I'm called Little Buttercup"

RECIT.

Hail, man-o'-war's men, safe-guards of your na-tion,

Here is an end, at last, of all pri-va-tion;

You've got your pay—spare all you can af-ford To wel-come Lit-tle But-ter-cup on board.

Attacca

ARIA
Allegretto

I'm

called Lit-tle But-ter-cup, dear Lit-tle But-ter-cup, Though I could nev-er tell why, But

still I'm called But-ter-cup, poor Lit-tle But-ter-cup, Sweet Lit-tle But-ter-cup I!

I've snuff and to - bac-cy, and ex-cel-lent jack-y, I've scis-sors, and watch-es, and

knives;   I've rib-bons and la-ces to set off the fa-ces Of pret-ty young

sweet-hearts and wives.   I've trea - cle and tof - fee, I've tea   and I've

cof - fee, Soft · tom-my and suc - cu-lent chops;   I've

chick-ens and co-nies, and pret-ty po - lo-nies, And ex - cel-lent pep-per-mint

drops. ___ Then buy of your But-ter-cup, dear Lit-tle But-ter-cup,

Sail-ors should nev-er be shy; So buy of your But-ter-cup,

poor Lit - tle But-ter-cup, Come, of your But-ter-cup buy. ___

BOAT.: . . . .Aye, Little Buttercup—— and well called——for you're the rosiest, the roundest, and the reddest beauty in all Spithead.

ALL:. . . . .Aye! Aye!

BUT.: . . . .Red, am I? and round—— and rosy! Maybe, for I have dissembled well! But hark ye, my merry friend——hast ever thought that beneath a gay and frivolous exterior there may lurk a canker-worm which is slowly but surely eating its way into one's very heart?

BOAT.: . . . .No, my lass, I can't say I've ever thought that.

(Enter Dick Deadeye. He pushes through sailors, and comes down.)

DICK: . . . .I've thought it often. *(All recoil from him.)*

BUT.: . . . .Yes, you look like it! What's the matter with the man? Isn't he well?

BOAT.: . . . .Don't take no heed of *him;* that's only poor Dick Deadeye.

DICK: . . . .I say—— it's a beast of a name, ain't it. Dick Deadeye.

BUT.: . . . .It's not a nice name.

DICK: . . . .I'm ugly too, ain't I?

BUT.: . . . .You are certainly plain.

DICK: . . . .And I'm three-cornered too, ain't I?

BUT.: . . . .You are rather triangular.

DICK: . . . .Ha! Ha! That's it. I'm ugly, and they hate me for it; for you all hate me, don't you?

ALL: . . . .We do!

DICK: . . . .There!

BOAT.: . . . .Well. Dick, we wouldn't go for to hurt any fellow creature's feelings, but you can't expect a chap with such a name as Dick Deadeye to be a popular character——now can you?

DICK: . . . .No.

BOAT.: . . . .It's asking too much, ain't it?

DICK: . . . .It is. From such a face and form as mine the noblest sentiments sound like the black utterances of a depraved imagination. It is human nature— I'm resigned.

No. 2ª Recitative— (Buttercup and Boatswain)

BUTTERCUP *(looking down hatchway)*

But tell me who's the youth whose falt'ring feet With dif-fi-cul-ty bear him on his course?

BOATSWAIN

That is the smartest lad in all the fleet, Ralph Rackstraw!

BUTTERCUP

Ralph! That name! Remorse! Remorse!

Attacca

(Enter Ralph from hatchway.)

No. 3 Madrigal—(Ralph and Chorus of Sailors)
"The nightingale"

RALPH

The night-in-gale Sighed for the moon's bright ray, And told his tale__ In his own mel-o-dious way. He

know the val-ue of a kind-ly cho-rus, But cho-rus-es yield lit-tle con-so-

la - tion When we have pain, and sor-row, too, be - fore us! I love—

BUTTERCUP (aside)

and love, a -las, a-bove my sta-tion! He loves, and loves a lass a-bove his

CHORUS unis.

sta - tion. Yes, yes, the lass is much a-bove his sta - tion.

Attacca

No. 3ª Ballad—(Ralph and Chorus of Sailors)
"A maiden fair to see"

Andante moderato

RALPH

maid-en fair to see, The pearl of min-strel-sy, A bud of blush-ing beau-ty; For

whom proud no-bles sigh, And with each oth-er vie To do her me-nial's du-ty. To

CHORUS

do her me-nial's du-ty.

RALPH

A suit-or, low-ly born, With

hope-less pas-sion torn, And poor, be-yond de - ny - ing, Has

dared for her to pine, At whose ex-alt-ed shrine A world of wealth is

CHORUS

sigh-ing. A world of wealth is sigh-ing.

RALPH

Un-learn-ed he in aught Save

that which love has taught (For love had been his tu - tor); Oh,

(Exit Buttercup.)

BOAT.: . . . .Ah, my poor lad, you've climbed too high; our worthy captain's child won't have nothin' to say to a poor chap like you. Will she, lads?

ALL: . . . . . .No, no!

DICK: . . . .No, no, captain's daughters don't marry foremast hands.

ALL. . . . . .*(recoiling from him)*: Shame! shame!

BOAT.: . . . .Dick Deadeye, them sentiments o' yourn are a disgrace to our common natur.'

RALPH: . . .But it's a strange anomaly that the daughter of a man who hails from the quarterdeck may not love another who lays out on the fore-yard arm. For a man is but a man, whether he hoists his flag at the main truck or his slacks on the main deck.

ALL: . . . .Aye! aye!

DICK: . . . .Ah, it's a queer world!

RALPH: . . .Dick Deadeye, I have no desire to press hardly on you, but such a revolutionary sentiment is enough to make an honest sailor shudder. *(All shudder.)*

BOAT.: . . . .My lads, our gallant captain has come on deck; let us greet him as so brave an officer and so gallant a seaman deserves.

(Enter Captain Corcoran.)

No. 4 Recit. and Song—(Captain Corcoran and Chorus of Sailors)
"My gallant crew"

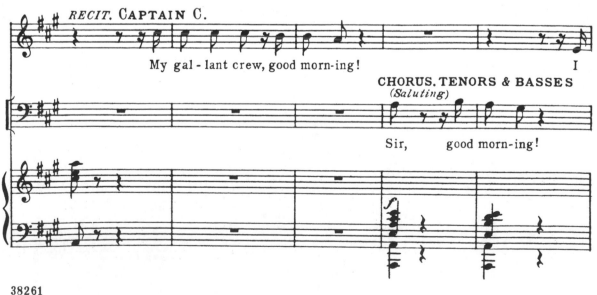

hope you're all quite well.
(As before)
I am in
Quite well, and you, sir?
rea-son-a-ble health, and hap-py To meet you all once more.
p
f
CHORUS
(As before)
You do us proud, sir!
ff
CAPTAIN C.
1. I

24

38261

be it un-der-stood, He com-mands a ___ right good crew.
thinks it on-ly right To re-turn the ___ com-pli-ment.

la-ted to a peer, I can hand, reef, and steer, Or ship a sel-va-
lan-guage or a-buse, I nev-er, nev-er use, What-ev-er the e-mer-gen-

gee; I am nev-er known to quail At the fu-ry of a gale, And I'm
cy; Though "both-er it" I may ___ Oc-ca-sion-al-ly say, I

26

38261

(*Exeunt all but Captain. Enter Buttercup.*)

38261

No. 4ª Recit.—(Buttercup and Captain Corcoran)

BUTTERCUP

Sir, you are sad! The si-lent e - lo-quence Of yonder tear, that trembles on your eye-lash,

Pro-claims a sor-row far more deep than common; Con-fide in me—fear not—I am a moth-er!

CAPTAIN C.

Yes, Lit-tle But-ter-cup, I'm sad and sor - ry,

My daugh-ter, Jo-se-phine, the fair-est flower That ev - er blos-somed on an-ces-tral

No. 5 Ballad– (Josephine)
"Sorry her lot"

(Enter Josephine, twining some flowers which she carries in a small basket.)

lot ___ who loves too well, Heav-y the heart ___ that hopes but vain - ly, Sad ___ are the sighs that own the spell Ut-tered by eyes ___ that speak too plain - ly. Sor-ry her lot ___ who loves too well, Heav-y the heart that hopes but vain - ly.

Un poco animato

Heav-y the sor-row that bows __ the head When love is a-live __ and hope __ is dead! When love is a-live and hope _____ is dead!

Andante

Sad is the hour __ when sets the sun— Dark is the night __ to earth's poor daugh-ters, When __ to the ark the

wea-ried one Flies from the emp - ty waste of wa - ters.

Sad is the hour— when sets the sun— Dark is the night to earth's poor

Un poco animato

rall.

daugh-ters. Heav - y the sor - row that bows — the

head When love is a - live — and hope — is dead! When

cresc.

dim. *p*

love — is a - live and hope — is dead!

colla voce

(Enter Captain.)

CAPT.: . . . .My child, I grieve to see that you are a prey to melancholy. You should look your best today, for Sir Joseph Porter, K.C.B., will be here this afternoon to claim your promised hand.

JOSEPHINE:.Ah, father, your words cut me to the quick. I can esteem — reverence — venerate Sir Joseph, for he is a great and good man; but oh, I cannot love him! My heart is already given.

CAPT. . . . .*(aside)*: It is then as I feared. *(Aloud.)* Given? And to whom? Not to some gilded lordling?

JOSEPHINE:.No, father — the object of my love is no lordling. Oh, pity me, for he is but a humble sailor on board your own ship!

CAPT.: . . . .Impossible!

JOSEPHINE:.Yes, it is true — too true.

CAPT.: . . . .A common sailor? Oh fie!

JOSEPHINE:.I blush for the weakness that allows me to cherish such a passion. I hate myself when I think of the depth to which I have stooped in permitting myself to think tenderly of one so ignobly born, but I love him! I love him! I love him! *(Weeps.)*

CAPT.: . . . .Come, my child, let us talk this over. In a matter of the heart I would not coerce my daughter — I attach but little value to rank or wealth, but the line must be drawn somewhere. A man in that station may be brave and worthy, but at every step he would commit solecisms that society would never pardon.

JOSEPHINE:.Oh, I have thought of this night and day. But fear not, father: I have a heart, and therefore I love; but I am your daughter, and therefore I am proud. Though I carry my love with me to the tomb, he shall never, never know it.

CAPT.: . . . .You *are* my daughter after all. But see, Sir Joseph's barge approaches, manned by twelve trusty oarsmen and accompanied by the admiring crowd of sisters, cousins, and aunts that attend him wherever he goes. Retire, my daughter, to your cabin — take this, his photograph, with you — it may help to bring you to a more reasonable frame of mind.

JOSEPHINE:.My own thoughtful father!

(Exit Josephine. Captain remains and ascends the poop-deck.)

No. 6 Barcarolle — (Sir Joseph's Female Relatives, *off-stage*)
"Over the bright blue sea"

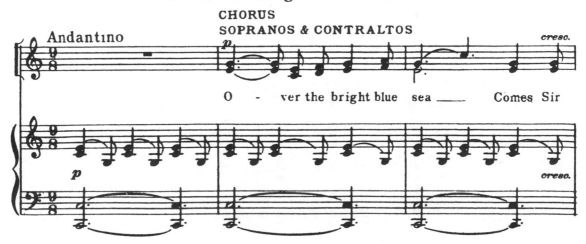

Jo - - seph Por-ter, K. C. B.; Wher - ev - - er he may go, — Bang - bang, the loud nine-pound-ers go!

Shout — o'er the bright blue sea — For Sir Jo-seph Por - ter, K. C.

B. Shout o'er the bright blue sea — For Sir Jo-seph Por-ter, K. C.

B. For Sir Jo-seph Por-ter, K. C. B. ——

(During No.6, the crew have entered on tiptoe, listening attentively to the song.)
38261

No. 7 — (Chorus of Sailors and Sir Joseph's Female Relatives)
"Sir Joseph's barge is seen"

Allegretto come I^{ma}

TENORS

p

Sir Jo-seph's barge is seen, And its crowd of blush-ing

BASSES

Sir Jo-seph's barge is seen, And its crowd of blush-ing

pp staccato

beau-ty, We hope he'll find us clean, And at-ten-tive to our

beau-ty, We hope he'll find us clean, And at-ten-tive to our

p

du-ty. We sail, we sail the o-cean blue, And our sau-cy ship's a

p

du-ty. We sail, we sail the o-cean blue, And our sau-cy ship's a

are so smart as we are.

are so smart as we are.

(Enter SIR JOSEPH'S FEMALE RELATIVES. *They*

dance around stage.)

SOPS. & ALTOS

Gai - ly

trip - ping, Light - ly— skip - ping, Flock the— maid - ens to— the—

ship - ping; Gai - ly_ trip - ping, Light - ly_ skip - ping, Flock the_

maid - ens to_ the ship - ping.

TENORS & BASSES

Flags, and guns, and pen - nants dip - ping, All the

Sail - ors_ spright - ly, **Al** - ways

la - dies love the ship - ping.

right - ly Wel - come la - dies so po - lite - ly.

TENORS & BASSES - - - - - - ly,

ly,

so po-lite - ly. Gai-ly trip-ping, Light-ly

most po-lite - ly. Gai-ly trip-ping, Light-ly

skip-ping, Sail-ors al-ways wel-come la-dies most po-lite - ly.

skip-ping, Sail-ors al-ways wel-come la-dies most po-lite - ly.

No. 8-(Capt. Corcoran, Sir Joseph, Cousin Hebe, and Chorus)
"Now give three cheers"

we are his sis-ters and his cous-ins and his aunts!

SOPS. & ALTOS

And we are his sis-ters and his

TENORS & BASSES

And they are his sis-ters and his

cresc.

His sis-ters and his cous-ins and his aunts!

cous-ins and his aunts, His sis-ters and his cous-ins and his aunts!

cous-ins and his aunts, His sis-ters and his cous-ins and his aunts!

f

SIR JOSEPH

When at an-chor here I ride, My bo-som swells with

p

COUSIN HEBE

pride, And I snap my fin-gers at a foe-man's taunts. And so do his sis-ters and his

No. 9 Song–(Sir Joseph and Chorus)
"When I was a lad"

Queen's Na - vee.
Queen's Na - vee.

He pol - ished up that han - dle so care - ful - lee, That
He cop - ied all the let - ters in a hand so free, That

He pol - ished up that han - dle so care - ful - lee, That
He cop - ied all the let - ters in a hand so free, That

SIR JOSEPH

3. In
4. Of

now he is the rul - er of the Queen's Na - vee.
now he is the rul - er of the Queen's Na - vee.

now he is the rul - er of the Queen's Na - vee.
now he is the rul - er of the Queen's Na - vee.

serv - ing writs I made such a name That an ar - ti - cled clerk I
leg - al knowl - edge I ac - quired such a grip That they took me in - to the

38261

SIR JOSEPH

5. I grew so rich that I was sent By a
6. Now lands-men all, who-ev-er you may be, If you

pock - et bor-ough in - to Par - lia - ment. I
want to rise to the top of the tree, If your

al - ways vot - ed at my par - ty's call, And I
soul is - n't fet - tered to an of - fice stool, Be

nev - er thought of think - ing for my - self at all.
care - ful to be guid - ed by this gold - en rule—

CHORUS

He
Be

He
Be

38261

thought so lit-tle, they re-ward-ed he, By
close to your desks and nev-er go to sea, And you

thought so lit-tle, they re-ward-ed he, By
close to your desks and nev-er go to sea, And you

mak-ing him the rul-er of the Queen's Na-vee.
all__ may be rul-ers of the

mak-ing him the rul-er of the Queen's Na-vee.
all__ may be rul-ers of the

Queen's Na-vee.

Queen's Na-vee.

SIR JOSEPH: . .You've a remarkably fine crew, Captain Corcoran.

CAPT.: . . . .It <u>is</u> a fine crew, Sir Joseph.

SIR JOSEPH. . .(*examining a very small midshipman*): A British sailor is a splendid fellow, Captain Corcoran.

CAPT.: . . . .A splendid fellow indeed, Sir Joseph.

SIR JOSEPH: . .I hope you treat your crew kindly, Captain Corcoran.

CAPT.: . . . .Indeed I hope so, Sir Joseph.

SIR JOSEPH: . .Never forget that they are the bulwarks of England's greatness, Captain Corcoran.

CAPT.: . . . .So I have always considered them, Sir Joseph.

SIR JOSEPH: . .No bullying, I trust—— no strong language of any kind, eh?

CAPT.: . . . .Oh, never, Sir Joseph.

SIR JOSEPH: . .What, <u>never</u>?

CAPT.: . . . .Well! hardly ever, Sir Joseph. They are an excellent crew, and do their work thoroughly without it.

SIR JOSEPH: . .Don't patronize them, sir—— pray don't patronize them.

CAPT.: . . . .Certainly not, Sir Joseph.

SIR JOSEPH: . .That you are their Captain is an accident of birth. I cannot permit these noble fellows to be patronized because an accident of birth has placed you above them and them below you.

CAPT.: . . . .I am the last person to insult a British sailor, Sir Joseph.

SIR JOSEPH: . .You are the last person who did, Captain Corcoran. Desire that splendid seaman to step forward:

(Dick comes forward.)

SIR JOSEPH: . .No, no, the other splendid seaman.

CAPT.: . . . .Ralph Rackstraw, three paces to the front—— march!

SIR JOSEPH. . .(*sternly*): If what?

CAPT.: . . . .I beg your pardon—— I don't think I understand you.

SIR JOSEPH: . .If you <u>please</u>.

CAPT.: . . . .Oh, yes, of course. If you please. (*Ralph steps forward.*)

SIR JOSEPH: . .You're a remarkably fine fellow.

RALPH: . . .Yes, your honour.

SIR JOSEPH: . .And a first-rate seaman, I'll be bound.

RALPH: . . .There's not a smarter topman in the navy, your honour, though I say it who shouldn't.

SIR JOSEPH: . .Not at all. Proper self-respect, nothing more Can you dance a hornpipe?

RALPH: . . .No, your honour.

SIR JOSEPH: . .That's a pity; all sailors should dance hornpipes. I will teach you one this evening, after dinner. Now tell **me**—— don't be afraid—— how does your Captain treat you, eh?

RALPH: . . .A better Captain doesn't walk the deck, your honour.

ALL: . . . . .Aye! Aye!

SIR JOSEPH: . .**Good.** I like to hear you speak well of your commanding officer; I dare say he doesn't deserve it, but still it does you credit. Can you sing?

RALPH: . . .I can hum a little, your honour.

SIR JOSEPH: . .Then hum this at your leisure. (*Giving him MS. music.*) It is a song that I have composed for the use of the Royal Navy. It is designed to encourage independence of thought and action in the lower branches of the service, and to teach the principle that a British sailor is any man's equal, excepting mine. Now, Captain Corcoran, a word with you in your cabin on a tender and sentimental subject.

CAPT.: . . . .Aye, aye, Sir Joseph. (*Crossing.*) Boatswain, in commemoration of this joyous occasion, see that extra grog is served out to the ship's company at seven bells.

BOAT.: . . . .Beg pardon. If what, your honour?

CAPT.: . . . .If what? I don't think I understand you.

BOAT.: . . . .If you *please*, your honour.

CAPT.: . . . .What!

SIR JOSEPH: . .The gentleman is quite right. If you <u>please</u>.

CAPT. . . . .(*stamping his foot impatiently*): If you *please!* (*Exit.*)

No. 9ª – (Sir Joseph, Cousin Hebe, Female Relatives and Sailors)
"For I hold that on the seas"

reck-ons up by doz-ens, and his aunts! _____

reck-ons up by doz-ens, and his aunts! _____

(Exeunt Sir Joseph and Relatives.)

BOAT.: . . . .Ah! Sir Joseph's a true gentleman, courteous and considerate to the very humblest.

RALPH:. . .True, Boatswain, but we are not the very humblest. Sir Joseph has explained our true position to us. As he says, a British seaman is any man's equal excepting his; and if Sir Joseph says that, is it not our duty to believe him?

ALL:. . . . .Well spoke! Well spoke!

DICK: . . . .You're on a wrong tack, and so is he. He means well, but he don't know. When people have to obey other people's orders, equality's out of the question.

ALL . . . . .*(recoiling)*: Horrible! Horrible!

BOAT.: . . . .Dick Deadeye, if you go for to infuriate this here ship's company too far, I won't answer for being able to hold 'em in. I'm shocked! That's what I am — shocked!

RALPH: . . .Messmates, my mind's made up. I'll speak to the captain's daughter, and tell her, like an honest man, of the honest love I have for her.

ALL: . . . .Aye, aye!

RALPH: . . .Is not my love as good as another's? Is not my heart as true as another's? Have I not hands and eyes and ears and limbs like another?

ALL: . . . .Aye, aye!

RALPH: . . .True, I lack birth —

BOAT.: . . . .You've a berth on board this very ship.

RALPH:. . .Well said — I had forgotten that. Messmates — what do you say? Do you approve my determination?

ALL: . . . .We do.

DICK: . . . .I don't.

BOAT.: . . . .What is to be done with this here hopeless chap? Let us sing him the song that Sir Joseph has kindly composed for us. Perhaps it will bring this here miserable creetur to a proper state of mind.

No. 10 Glee—(Ralph, Boatswain, Carpenter's Mate, and Chorus of Sailors)
"A British tar"

60

38261

(All dance off except Ralph, who remains, leaning pensively against bulwark.)

(Enter Josephine from cabin.)

JOSEPHINE: It is useless— Sir Joseph's attentions nauseate me. I know that he is a truly great and good man, for he told me so himself, but to me he seems tedious, fretful, and dictatorial. Yet his must be a mind of no common order, or he would not dare to teach my dear father to dance a hornpipe on the cabin table. *(Sees Ralph.)* Ralph Rackstraw! *(Overcome by emotion.)*

RALPH: . . . Aye, lady— no other than poor Rackstraw!

JOSEPHINE: *(aside)*: How my heart beats! *(Aloud.)* And why poor, Ralph?

RALPH: . . . I am poor in the essence of happiness, lady— rich only in never-ending unrest. In me there meet a combination of antithetical elements which are at eternal war with one another. Driven hither by objective influences—— thither by subjective emotions—— wafted one moment into blazing day, by mocking hope—— plunged the next into the Cimmerian darkness of tangible despair, I am but a living ganglion of irreconcilable antagonisms. I hope I make myself clear, lady?

JOSEPHINE: Perfectly. *(Aside.)* His simple eloquence goes to my heart. Oh, if I dared—— but no, the thought is madness! *(Aloud.)* Dismiss these foolish fancies, they torture you but needlessly. Come, make one effort.

RALPH.. . . *(aside)*: I will— one. *(Aloud.)* Josephine!

JOSEPHINE.. *(indignantly)*: Sir!

RALPH: . . . Aye, even though Jove's armoury were launched at the head of the audacious mortal whose lips, unhallowed by relationship, dared to breathe that precious word, yet would I breathe it once, and then perchance be silent evermore. Josephine, in one brief breath I will concentrate the hopes, the doubts, the anxious fears of six weary months. Josephine, I am a British sailor, and I love you!

JOSEPHINE: Sir, this audacity! *(Aside.)* Oh, my heart, my beating heart. *(Aloud.)* This unwarrantable presumption on the part of a common sailor! *(Aside.)* Common! oh, the irony of the word! *(Crossing, aloud.)* Oh, sir, you forget the disparity in our ranks.

RALPH: . . . I forget nothing, haughty lady. I love you desperately, my life is in your hand: I lay it at your feet! Give me hope, and what I lack in education and polite accomplishments, that I will endeavour to acquire. Drive me to despair, and in death alone I shall look for consolation. I am proud and cannot stoop to implore. I have spoken, and I wait your word.

JOSEPHINE: You shall not wait long. Your proffered love I haughtily reject. Go, sir, and learn to cast your eyes on some village maiden in your own poor rank— they should be lowered before your captain's daughter.

No. 11 Duet — (Josephine and Ralph)
"Refrain, audacious tar"

Allegro con brio

JOSEPHINE

Re-frain, au - da - cious tar, Your suit from press - ing, Re - mem - ber what you are, And whom ad - dress - ing! Re - frain, au - da - cious tar, Your suit from press - ing, Re - mem - ber what you are, And whom ad - dress - ing! Re - frain, au - da - cious tar, Re - mem - ber what you are, I'd

64

38261

Tempo I

JOSEPHINE

dore her. Re - frain, au - da - cious tar, Your suit from

press - ing!

RALPH

Proud la - dy, have your way, Un - feel - ing beau - ty! My

più lento

I'd

laugh my rank to scorn In u - nion ho - ly, Were he more high-ly born Or

heart, with an-guish torn, Bows down be - fore her; She laughs my love to scorn, Yet

I more low - ly.

I a - dore her.

(Exit Josephine into cabin.)

38261

No. 12 Finale—(ACT I)
"Can I survive this overbearing?"

Allegretto moderato

RALPH RECIT.

Can I sur-vive this o-ver-bear-ing? Or live a life of mad des-pair-ing? My prof-fer'd love despis'd, re-ject-ed? No, no, it's not to be ex-pect-ed!

RALPH (Enter Sailors, Hebe, Relatives, and Buttercup.)

Allegro con brio Mess-mates, a-hoy! Come here! Come here!

SOPS. & ALTOS
Aye, aye, my boy, What cheer, what cheer? Now tell us, pray, With-out de-

TENORS & BASSES
Aye, aye, my boy, What cheer, what cheer? Now tell us, pray, With-out de-

RALPH Un poco più lento

My friends, my leave of life I'm tak - ing, For oh, my heart, my heart is break-ing; When I am gone, oh prithee, tell The maid that, as I died, I loved her well!

CHORUS *(turning away, weeping)*

Of life, a - las! his leave he's tak - ing, For

Of life, a - las! his leave he's tak - ing, For

ah! his faith-ful heart is break - ing. When he is gone we'll sure - ly

ah! his faith-ful heart is break - ing. When he is gone we'll sure - ly

(During Chorus. Boatswain loads pistol and hands it to Ralph.)

that, as he died, he loved her well! RALPH

tell The maid,   as he died, he loved her well! Be warned, my

tell The maid,   as he died, he loved her well!

mess-mates all Who love in rank a-bove you— For Jo-seph-ine I

(Puts pistol to his head.
All the sailors stop their ears. Enter Josephine, on deck.)
JOSEPHINE. *RECIT.*

Tutti. CHORUS
SOPRANOS & CONTRALTOS

fall!   Ah! stay your hand! I love you! TENORS & BASSES

Ah! stay your hand—she loves you!

RALPH JOSEPHINE SOPRANOS & CONTRALTOS

TENORS & BASSES

Loves me?   Loves you! Yes! Yes! Ah yes! she loves you!

79

38261

82

38261

man Shall make us one At half-past ten, And then we can Re-turn, for none, none,

man Shall make them one At half-past ten, And then they can Re-turn, for none, none,

man Shall make us one At half-past ten, And then we can Re-turn, for none, none,

man Shall make them one At half-past ten, And then they can Re-turn, for none, none,

man Shall make them one At half-past ten, And then they can Re-turn, for none, none,

man Shall make them one At half-past ten, And then they can Re-turn, for none, none,

man Shall make them one At half-past ten, And then they can Re-turn, for none, none,

part us then!

part them then!

part us then!

none Can part them then!

none Can part them then!

none Can part them then!

none Can part them then!

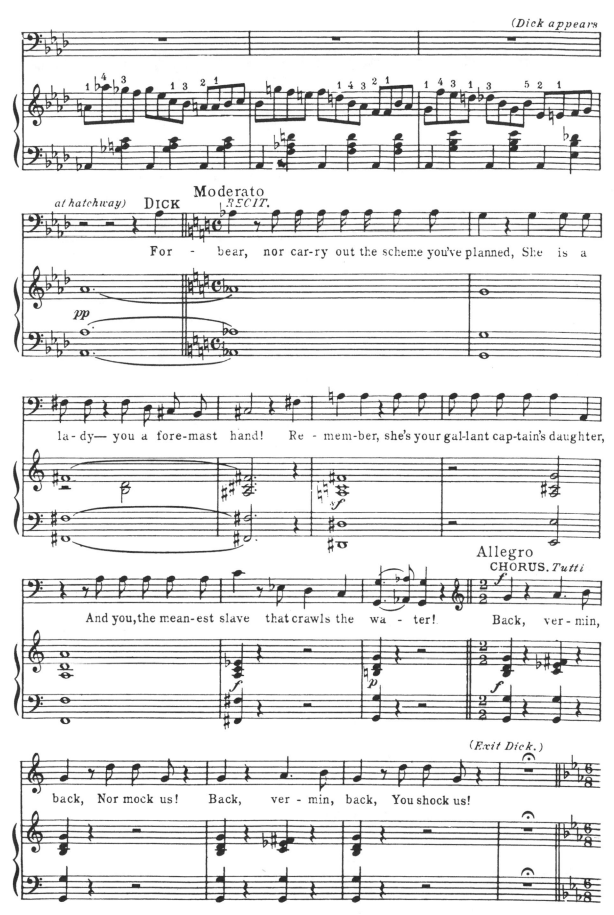

(Dick appears at hatchway) DICK

Moderato RECIT.

For- bear, nor car-ry out the scheme you've planned, She is a la-dy— you a fore-mast hand! Re- mem-ber, she's your gal-lant cap-tain's daughter, And you, the mean-est slave that crawls the wa- ter!

Allegro CHORUS. Tutti

Back, ver-min, back, Nor mock us! Back, ver- min, back, You shock us!

(Exit Dick.)

38261

Allegro con brio

CHORUS

Let's give three cheers for the sail-or's bride, Who

casts all thought of rank a-side—And gives up home and for-tune, too, For the

hon - est love of a sail-or true! Tra, la, la, la, la, la, la, la, la,

la, la,

give three cheers for the sail-or's bride, Who casts all thought of rank a-side—And

give three cheers for the sail-or's bride, Who casts all thought of rank a-side—And

gives up home and for-tune, too, For the hon-est love of a sail-or true!

gives up home and for-tune, too, For the hon-est love of a sail-or true!

JOSEPHINE, COUSIN HEBE, BUTTERCUP
Vivace

SOPRANOS & CONTRALTOS UNISON
For a   Brit-ish tar is a soar-ing soul As

free as a moun-tain bird; His en-er-get-ic fist should be read-y to re-sist A

dic-ta-to-rial **word!** His eyes should flash with an in - born fire, His

brow with scorn be wrung; He nev-er should bow down to a dom-in-eer-ing frown, Or the

tang of a ty-rant tongue.

RALPH, BOATSWAIN, & CARPENTER

TENORS & BASSES UNISON
His nose should pant, and his lip should curl, His

cheeks should flame; and his brow should furl, His bos-om should heave, and his

cresc.

heart should glow, And his fist be ev-er read-y for a knock-down blow.

f

SOPS. & ALTOS

His foot should stamp, and his throat should growl, His

RALPH with TENORS

BOATSWAIN & CARPENTER with BASSES

His foot should stamp, and his throat should growl, His

ff

hair should twirl, and his face should scowl, His eyes should flash, and his breast pro-trude, And

hair should twirl, and his face should scowl, His eyes should flash, and his breast pro-trude, And

JOSEPHINE
this should be his cus-tom-a-ry at-ti-tude, His eyes should
COUSIN HEBE
this should be his cus-tom-a-ry at-ti-tude, His eyes should
RALPH
this should be his cus-tom-a-ry at-ti-tude, His eyes should
BOATSWAIN
this should be his cus-tom-a-ry at-ti-tude, His eyes should
CARPENTER
this should be his cus-tom-a-ry at-ti-tude, His eyes should
this should be his cus-tom-a-ry at-ti-tude, his
this should be his cus-tom-a-ry at-ti-tude, his
J.
flash, his breast pro-trude, His eyes
H.
flash, his breast pro-trude, His eyes
R.
flash, his breast pro-trude, His eyes
B.
flash, his breast pro-trude, His eyes
C.
flash, his breast pro-trude, His eyes
at-ti-tude, his at-ti-tude,
at-ti-tude, his at-ti-tude,

94

38261

(Pose)

J. And this his at - - ti - tude.

H. And this his at - - ti - tude.

R. And this his at - - ti - tude.

B. And this his at - - ti - tude.

C. And this his at - - ti - tude.

cus-tom-a-ry at - - - - - ti - tude.

cus-tom-a-ry at - - - - - ti - tude.

(All dance.)

rall.

END OF ACT I

CURTAIN

Entr'acte

ACT II

No. 13 Song— (Captain Corcoran)
"Fair moon, to thee I sing"

(Same Scene. Night. Moonlight. Captain discoverd singing, and accompanying himself on a guitar. Little Buttercup, seated on quarter-deck, gazing sentimentally at him.)

Fair moon, to thee I _ sing, Bright re-gent of the heav - ens,

Say, why is ev-'ry-thing_ Ei-ther at six-es or at sev - ens?

Say, why is ev-'ry - thing Ei-ther at six-es or at sev-ens? I have

lived hith-er-to   Free from the breath of

slan-der,   Be-loved by all my crew,   A

real-ly pop-u-lar com-mand-er. But now my kind-ly crew re-

bel,__ My daugh-ter to a tar is par-tial, Sir

Jo-seph storms, and, sad to tell, He threat-ens__ a court-

cresc.

38261

BUT.: . . . . .How sweetly he carols forth his melody to the unconscious moon! Of whom is he thinking? Of some high born beauty? It may be! Who is poor Little Buttercup that she should expect his glance to fall on one so lowly! And yet if he knew— if he only knew!

CAPT. . . . .(*coming down*): Ah! Little Buttercup, still on board? That is not quite right, little one. It would have been more respectable to have gone on shore at dusk.

BUT.. . . . . .True, dear captain— but the recollection of your sad, pale face seemed to chain me to the ship. I would fain see you smile before I go.

CAPT.: . . . .Ah! Little Buttercup, I fear it will be long before I recover my accus - tomed cheerfulness, for misfortunes crowd upon me, and all my old friends seem to have turned against me!

BUT.: . . . . .Oh, no— do not say "all," dear Captain. That were unjust to one, at least.

CAPT.: . . . .True, for you are staunch to me. (*Aside.*) If ever I gave my heart again, methinks it would be to such a one as this! (*Aloud.*) I am touched to the heart by your innocent regard for me, and were we differently situated, I think I could have returned it. But, as it is, I fear I can never be more to you than a friend.

BUT.: . . . . .I understand! You hold aloof from me because you are rich and lofty— and I, poor and lowly. But take care! The poor bumboat woman has gypsy blood in her veins, and she can read destinies.

CAPT.: . . . .Destinies!

BUT.: . . . . .There is a change in store for you!

CAPT.: . . . .A change!

BUT.: . . . . .Aye— be prepared!

No. 14 Duet— (Buttercup and Captain Corcoran)
"Things are seldom what they seem"

CAPTAIN C. *(puzzled)*

Jack-daws strut in pea-cock's feathers. Ver-y true, So they do.

BUTTERCUP

Black sheep dwell in ev - 'ry fold, All that glit - ters is not gold;

Storks turn out to be but logs, Bulls are but in - flat - ed frogs.

CAPTAIN C. *(puzzled)*   BUTTERCUP

So they be, Fre - quent - lee. Drops the wind and

stops the mill, Tur - bot is am - bi - tious brill; Gild the far-thing if you will,

CAPTAIN C. (*puzzled*)

Yet it is a far-thing still. Yes, I know, That is so.

Tho' to catch your drift I'm striv-ing, It is sha-dy— it is sha-dy;

I don't see at what you're driv-ing, Mys-tic la-dy— mys-tic la-dy.

BUTTERCUP (*aside*)

Stern con-vic-tion's o'er him steal-ing That the mys-tic

CAPTAIN C. (*aside*)

Stern con-vic-tion's o'er me steal-ing That the mys-tic

la - dy's deal - ing In o - rac - u - lar re - veal - ing.

la - dy's deal - ing In o - rac - u - lar re - veal - ing.

That is so!

Yes, I know—

CAPTAIN C.

Tho' I'm an - y -

thing but clev-er, I could talk like that for - ev-er: Once a cat was

BUTTERCUP

killed by care, On - ly brave de - serve the fair. Ver - y true,

That is so! I'll dis-sem-ble, I'll dis-

Yes, I know. Tho' a mys-tic tone you bor-row,

-sem-ble, Let him trem-ble! Let him trem-ble! Let him

I shall learn the truth with sor-row; Here to-day and

trem-ble! Yes, I know, That is so!

gone to-mor-row, Yes, I know, That is so!

(Exit Buttercup, melodramatically.)

CAPT.: . . . .Incomprehensible as her utterances are, I nevertheless feel that they are dictated by a sincere regard for me. But to what new misery is she referring? Time alone can tell.

(Enter Sir Joseph.)

SIR JOSEPH: . . .Captain Corcoran, I am much disappointed with your daughter. In fact, I don't think she will do.

CAPT.: . . . .She won't do, Sir Joseph!

SIR JOSEPH: . . .I'm afraid not. The fact is, that although I have urged my suit with as much eloquence as is consistent with an official utterance, I have done so hitherto without success. How do you account for this?

CAPT.: . . . .Really, Sir Joseph, I hardly know. Josephine is of course sensible of your condescension.

SIR JOSEPH: . . .She naturally would be.

CAPT.: . . . .But perhaps your exalted rank dazzles her.

SIR JOSEPH: . . .You think it does?

CAPT.: . . . .I can hardly say; but she is a modest girl, and her social position is far below your own. It may be that she feels she is not worthy of you.

SIR JOSEPH: . . .That is really a very sensible suggestion, and displays more knowledge of human nature than I had given you credit for.

CAPT.: . . . .See, she comes. If your lordship would kindly reason with her and assure her officially that it is a standing rule at the Admiralty that love levels all ranks, her respect for an official utterance might induce her to look upon your offer in its proper light.

SIR JOSEPH: . . .It is not unlikely. I will adopt your suggestion. But soft, she is here. Let us withdraw, and watch our opportunity.

(Enter Josephine from cabin. Sir Joseph and Captain retire.)

No. 15 Scena — (Josephine)
"The hours creep on apace"

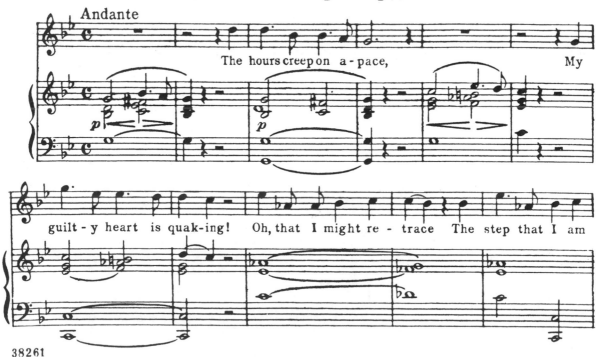

Andante

The hours creep on a-pace, My guilt-y heart is quak-ing! Oh, that I might re-trace The step that I am

taking. Its fol-ly it were ea-sy to be show-ing: What I am giv-ing up, and whith-er go - ing.

{On the one hand, papa's luxurious home,
Hung with ancestral armour and old} brasses,

{Carved oak and tapestry from distant Rome,
Rare "blue and white," Venetian finger-} glasses, {Rich Oriental rugs,
luxurious sofa,} pil-lows, And

ev-'ry-thing that is-n't old, from Gil-lows!

{And, on the other, a dark and dingy room
In some back street with stuffy children} crying,

Where organs yell, and clacking housewives fume, And clothes are hanging out all day a- dry-ing, With one cracked looking-glass to see your face in, And

dinner served up in a pudding- bas-in!

Allegro con spirito

cresc. molto

f

A sim - ple sail - or, low - ly born, Un-

let - tered and un - known, Who toils for bread from

ear - ly morn Till half the night has flown, Till

half the night has flown! No gold-en rank can he im-part, No

wealth of house or land, No for-tune, save his trust-y heart, And

hon - est, brown right hand, his trust-y heart, and brown right hand! And

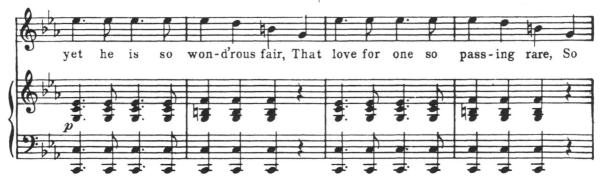

yet he is so won-d'rous fair, That love for one so pass-ing rare, So

peer-less in his man-ly beau-ty, Were lit-tle else than sol-emn du-ty, Were

112

38261

say, Which of you twain shall my poor heart ____ o - bey, my ____

heart o - bey, Which shall my heart, ____ my heart o -

bey!

(Sir Joseph and Captain enter.)

SIR JOSEPH:...Madam, it has been represented to me that you are appalled by my exalted rank. I desire to convey to you officially my assurance, that if your
hesitation is attributable to that circumstance, it is uncalled for.

JOSEPHINE:.Oh, then your lordship is of the opinion that married happiness is not inconsist-
ent with discrepancy in rank?

SIR JOSEPH:...I am officially of that opinion.

JOSEPHINE:.That the high and the lowly may be truly happy together, provided that they
truly love one another?

SIR JOSEPH: ...Madam, I desire to convey to you officially my opinion that love is a plat-
form upon which all ranks meet.

JOSEPHINE:.I thank you, Sir Joseph. I did hesitate, but I will hesitate no longer. *(Aside.)*
He little thinks how eloquently he has pleaded his rival's cause!

No. 16 Trio — (Josephine, Captain, and Sir Joseph)
"Never mind the why and wherefore"

Allegro vivace

Captain: 1. Nev - er mind the why and where-fore, Love can
Sir Joseph: 2. Nev - er mind the why and where-fore, Love can
Josephine: 3. Nev - er mind the why and where-fore, Love can

lev-el ranks, and there-fore, Though his Lord-ship's station's might-y, Though stu -
lev-el ranks, and there-fore, Though your nau - ti - cal re - la - tion In my
lev-el ranks, and there-fore I ad - mit the jur - is - dic - tion; Ab - ly

pen-dous be his brain, Though her tastes are mean and flight-y, And her
set could scarce-ly pass, Though you oc - cu-py a sta-tion In the
have you played your part, You have car-ried firm con-vic-tion To my

CAPTAIN C. & SIR JOSEPH *(each verse)*

for-tune poor__ and plain__
low-er mid - dle class__
hes-i - tat - ing heart.

Ring the mer - ry

bells on board-ship, Rend the air with warb-ling wild, For the u - nion

CAPTAIN C.
(each verse)

of his my Lord-ship With a hum-ble cap-tain's child, For a hum-ble cap-tain's

JOSEPHINE
(each verse)

SIR JOSEPH
(each verse)

daugh-ter, For a gal-lant cap-tain's daugh-ter, And a Lord who rules the

JOSEPHINE 3rd Verse

Let the air with joy be la-den,

CAPTAIN & SIR JOSEPH

Ring the mer-ry bells on board-ship,

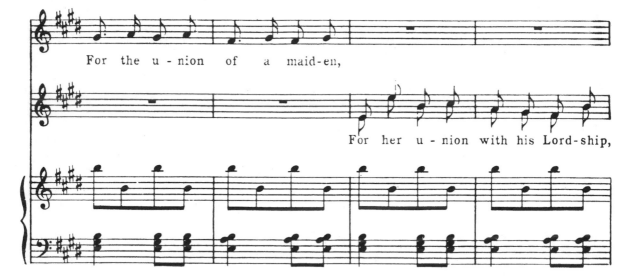

For the u-nion of a maid-en,

For her u-nion with his Lord-ship,

Rend with songs the air a-bove, For the man who owns her love,

Rend with songs the air a-bove, For the man who owns her love,

Rend with songs the air — a - bove, For the man who owns

Rend with songs the air a - bove, For the man who owns

her love.____

her love.____

(*Exit Josephine.*)

CAPT.: . . . .Sir Joseph, I cannot express to you my delight at the happy result of your eloquence. Your argument was unanswerable.

SIR JOSEPH: . . .Captain Corcoran, it is one of the happiest characteristics of this glorious country that official utterances are invariably regarded as unanswerable. (*Exit Sir Joseph.*)

CAPT.: . . . .At last my fond hopes are to be crowned. My only daughter is to be the bride of a Cabinet Minister. The prospect is Elysian.(*During this speech Dick Deadeye has entered.*)

DICK: . . . .Captain.

CAPT.: . . . .Deadeye! You here? Don't! (*Recoiling from him.*)

DICK: . . . .Ah, don't shrink from me, Captain. I'm unpleasant to look at, and my name's agin me, but I ain't as bad as I seem.

CAPT.: . . . .What would you with me?

DICK . . . .(*mysteriously*): I'm come to give you warning.

CAPT.: . . . .Indeed! Do you propose to leave the Navy then?

DICK: . . . .No, no, you misunderstand me; listen!

No. 17 Duet – (Captain and Dick Deadeye)
"Kind Captain, I've important information"

A - bout a cer - tain in - ti - mate re - la - - tion, Sing

CAPTAIN

The

hey, the mer - ry maid - en and the tar.

mer - ry, mer - ry maid - en, The mer - ry, mer - ry maid - en, Sing

The mer - ry, mer - ry maid - en, The mer - ry, mer - ry

hey, the mer - ry maid - en __ and the tar.

maid - en, The maid - en and the tar.

CAPTAIN

2. Good

fel - low, in con - un - drums you are speak - ing, Sing hey, the mys - tic

sail - or that you are, The an - swer to them vain - ly I am

seek - ing, Sing hey, the mer - ry maid - en and the

124

38261

much too mer - ry maid - en___ and the tar.

maid - en, The maid - en___ and the tar.

CAPTAIN

4. Good

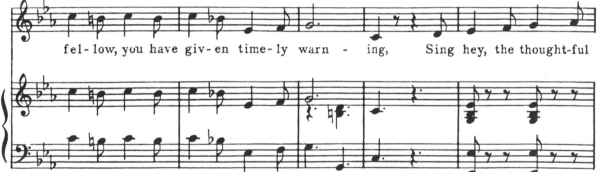

fel - low, you have giv-en time-ly warn - ing, Sing hey, the thought-ful

sail - or that you are; I'll talk to Mas-ter Rack-straw in the

(*Producing a*

morn - ing, Sing hey, the cat - o'-nine - tails and the tar.

"cat.")

The mer - ry cat - o' - nine - tails, The mer - ry cat - o' -

The mer - ry cat - o' - nine - tails, The

nine - tails, The mer - ry cat - o' - nine - tails and the tar!

mer - ry cat, The mer - ry cat - o' - nine - tails and the tar!

CAPT.: . . . .Dick Deadeye — I thank you for your warning — I will at once take means to arrest their flight. This boat cloak will afford me ample disguise — So! (*Envelops himself in a mysterious cloak, holding it before his face.*)

DICK: . . . .Ha, ha! They are foiled — foiled — foiled!

(*Enter Crew on tiptoe, with Ralph and Boatswain meeting Josephine, who enters from Cabin on tiptoe, with bundle of necessaries, and accompanied by Little Buttercup.*)

No. 18 Soli and Chorus
"Carefully on tiptoe stealing"

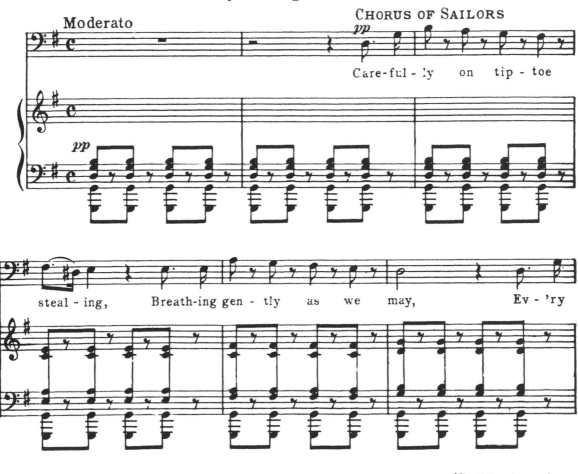

DICK

CHORUS

me! Why, what was that? Si-lent be, It was the cat! It

CAPTAIN *(aside)*

CHORUS

was, it was the cat! They're right, it was the cat! Pull a-

shore in fash-ion stead-y, Hy-men will de-fray the fare, For a

(Captain stamps.)

cler-gy-man is read-y To — u - nite the hap-py pair! Good-ness

me,   Why, what was that?   Si-lent be,   A-gain the

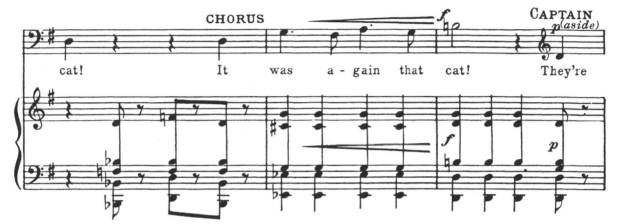

CHORUS   **CAPTAIN** (aside)

cat!   It   was   a-gain   that   cat!   They're

JOSEPHINE

Ev-'ry step with cau - tion

RALPH

Ev-'ry step with cau - tion

right,   it was the cat!   with cau - tion

DICK

Ev-'ry step with cau - tion

Where you may be go - ing With these sons of the brine. For my

ex - cel - lent crew, Though foes they could thump an - y, Are scarce - ly fit com-pa-ny, My

CHORUS

daugh-ter, for you. Now, hark at that, do! Though foes we could thump an - y, We're

RALPH

scarce-ly fit com-pa-ny For a la - dy like you! Proud

off - i - cer, that haught-y lip un - curl! Vain

man, sup-press that su - per - cil - ious sneer, For I have

dared to love your match less girl, A

fact well known to all my mess - mates here! Oh, hor-ror!

CAPTAIN

JOSEPHINE *p*

He, hum-ble, poor, and low - ly born, The mean - est in the

RALPH *p*

I, hum-ble, poor, and low - ly born, The mean - est in the

p

port div-i-sion— The butt of e-pau-let-ted scorn— The

port div-i-sion— The butt of e-pau-let-ted scorn— The

mark of quar-ter-deck de-ri-sion—Has dared to raise his

mark of quar-ter-deck de-ri-sion—Have dared to raise my

worm-y eyes A-bove the dust to which you'd mould him, In

worm-y eyes A-bove the dust to which you'd mould me, In

135

38261

Moderato

he him-self has said it, And it's great-ly to his cred-it, That he
is an Eng-lish-man!
For he
That he is an Eng-lish-man!
That he is an Eng-lish-man!

might have been a Roo-sian. A French, or Turk, or Proo-sian, Or per-haps I-tal-i-
an!

TENORS & BASSES

But in spite of all temp-ta-tions To be-

Or per-haps I-tal-i-an!

long to oth-er nations, He re-mains an Eng-lish-man! He re-

mains an Eng - - - lish-man!

CHORUS OF MEN

f a tempo

For in spite of all temp-

ta-tions To be-long to oth-er nations, He re-mains an Eng-lish-

He re - mains an Eng - - - lish-man!

man! He re - mains an Eng - - - lish-man!

CAPTAIN (*trying to repress his anger*) (*During this, enter Cousin Hebe and*

In ut-ter-ing a re-pro-ba-tion To an-y Brit-ish

Female Relatives.)

tar, I try to speak with mod - e -ra-tion, But

you have gone too far. I'm ver-y sor-ry

to dis-par-age A hum - ble fore-mast lad, But to

seek your cap-tain's child in mar-riage—Why, dam-me, it's too

bear - ing! Don't go near him— don't go near him— He is

he said dam - me; he said dam - me, he said dam - me,

Yes, he said dam - me, dam - me, dam - me, dam - me,

swear - ing— he is swear - ing! My pain and my dis-

Yes, dam - me.

dam - me, Yes, dam - me.

SIR JOSEPH *(who has appeared on*

Moderato

p

the poop-deck)

tress, I find it is not ea - sy to ex - press; My a -

word of e-vil sense, Is whol-ly in-de-fen-s-ble.

Go, ri-bald, get you hence To your ca-bin with ce-le-ri-ty.

(Exit Captain,

This is the con-se-quence Of ill-ad-vised as-pe-ri-ty!

disgraced, followed by Josephine.)

SIR JOSEPH

For I'll

SOPRANOS & CONTRALTOS

This is the con-se-quence Of ill-ad-vised as-pe-ri-ty!

TENORS & BASSES

This is the con-se-quence Of ill-ad-vised as-pe-ri-ty!

teach you all, ere long, To re-frain from lan-guage

strong, For I hav-en't an-y sym-pa-thy for ill-bred taunts! No

HEBE

more have his sis-ters, nor his cou-sins, nor his aunts.

CHORUS

No

No

more have his sis-ters, nor his cou-sins, nor his aunts, No

more have his sis-ters, nor his cou-sins, nor his aunts, No

stringendo molto

sempre stringendo

cresc.

And it's

For he him-self has said it, And it's great-ly

For he him-self has said it, And it's great-ly

That he

to his cred-it, That he is an Eng-lish-man!

to his cred-it, That he is an Eng-lish-man!

That he is an Eng - - - lish-man!

That he is an Eng - - lish-man!

rall.

(Re-enter Josephine.)

SIR JOSEPH: . .Now, tell me, my fine fellow — for you <u>are</u> a fine fellow —

RALPH: . . .Yes, your honour.

SIR JOSEPH: . .How came your captain so far to forget himself? I am quite sure you had given him no cause for annoyance.

RALPH: . . .Please, your honour, it was thus-wise. You see, I'm only a top-man — a mere foremast hand —

SIR JOSEPH: . .Don't be ashamed of that. Your position as a top-man is a very exalted one.

RALPH: . . .Well, your honour, love burns as brightly in the fo'c's'le as it does on the quarter-deck, and Josephine is the fairest bud that ever blossomed upon the tree of a poor fellow's wildest hopes.

(Josephine rushes to Ralph's arms.)

JOSEPHINE: .Darling! *(Sir Joseph horrified.)*

RALPH: . . .She is the figurehead of my ship of life — the bright beacon that guides me into my port of happiness — the rarest, the purest gem that ever sparkled on a poor but worthy fellow's trusting brow.

ALL: . . . .Very pretty, very pretty!

SIR JOSEPH: . .Insolent sailor, you shall repent this outrage. Seize him! *(Two Marines seize him and handcuff him.)*

JOSEPHINE: .Oh, Sir Joseph, spare him, for I love him tenderly.

SIR JOSEPH: . .Pray don't. I will teach this presumptuous mariner to discipline his affections. Have you such a thing as a dungeon on board?

ALL: . . . . .We have!

DICK: . . . .They have!

SIR JOSEPH: .Then load him with chains and take him there at once.

No. 19 Octet and Chorus
"Farewell, my own!"

Fare-well, my own, Light of my life, fare-

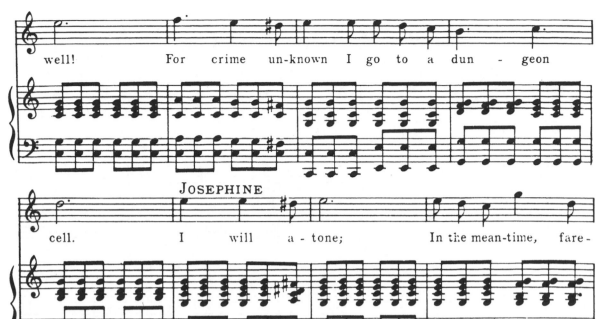

For crime un-known I go to a dun - geon cell. I will a - tone; In the mean-time, fare-

JOSEPHINE

well! And all a - lone Re-joice in your dun - geon cell!

SIR JOSEPH

A bone, a bone I'll pick with this sail - or

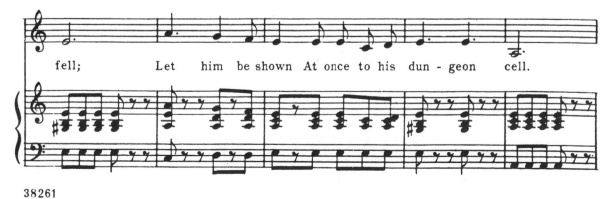

fell; Let him be shown At once to his dun - geon cell.

38261

148

COUSIN HEBE

p

He'll hear no tone ___ Of the maid-en he loves so well!

DICK DEADEYE

p

He'll hear no tone ___ Of the maid-en he loves so well!

BOATSWAIN

p

He'll hear no tone ___ Of the maid-en he loves so well!

p **CARPENTER**

He'll hear no tone ___ Of the maid-en he loves so well!

No tel - e - phone Com-mu-ni-cates with his cell!

No tel - e - phone Com-mu-ni-cates with his cell!

No tel - e - phone Com-mu-ni-cates with his cell!

No tel - e - phone Com-mu-ni-cates with his cell!

BUTTERCUP *(mysteriously)*

But when is known ___ The se-cret I have to tell,

Wide will be thrown The door of his dun-geon cell.

mf JOSEPHINE
Fare - well, my own, Light of my life, fare - well! And all a-

mf COUSIN HEBE
He'll hear no tone Of her he loves so well! Let him be

mf BUTTERCUP
He'll hear no tone Of her he loves so well! For crime un-

mf RALPH
Fare - well, my own, Light of my life, fare - well! For crime un-

mf SIR JOSEPH
He'll hear no tone Of her he loves so well! Let him be

mf DEADEYE
He'll hear no tone Of her he loves so well! For crime un-

mf BOATSWAIN
He'll hear no tone Of her he loves so well! For crime un-

mf CARPENTER
He'll hear no tone Of her he loves so well! For crime un-

CHORUS. SOPRANOS & CONTRALTOS
p
For crime un-

TENORS & BASSES
p
For crime un-

easy to express; My amazement, my surprise, Again you may discover from my eyes!

CHORUS
How terrible the aspect of his

How terrible the aspect of his

BUTTERCUP
Hold!

eyes!

eyes!

Ere upon your loss You lay much stress, A long concealed crime I would confess!

No. 20 Song—(Buttercup and Chorus)
"A many years ago"

charm-ing,   She prac-tised ba - by-farm-ing,   A man-y years a-

charm-ing,   She prac-tised ba - by-farm-ing,   A man-y years a-

BUTTERCUP

Two ten-der babes I nuss'd: One was of low con-di-tion,   The

go.

go.

oth-er, up-per crust,   A re-gu-lar pa-tri-cian.

Now, this is the po-

Now, this is the po-

cresc.

sf   p

si - tion: One was of low con - di - tion, The oth - er a pa -

si - tion: One was of low con - di - tion, The oth - er a pa -

tri - cian, A man - y years a - go.

tri - cian, A man - y years a - go.

BUTTERCUP

Oh, bit - ter is my cup! How - e - ver could I

do it? I mixed those chil - dren up, And not a crea - ture

knew it!

How - ev - er could you do it? Some day, no doubt, you'll

How - ev - er could you do it? Some day, no doubt, you'll

In

rue it, Al-though no crea-ture knew it, So man-y years a - go.

rue it, Al-though no crea-ture knew it, So man-y years a - go.

time each lit - tle waif For - sook his fos - ter

moth-er, The well-born babe was Ralph— Your cap-tain was the

cresc.

SIR JOSEPH:...Then I am to understand **that Captain** Corcoran and Ralph were exchanged in childhood's happy **hours** —— that Ralph is really the Captain, and the Captain is Ralph?

BUT.:.....That is the idea I intended to convey, officially!

SIR JOSEPH:...And very well you have conveyed it, Miss Buttercup!

BUT.:.....Aye! Aye! Yer 'onour.

SIR JOSEPH:...Dear me! Let them appear before me at once!

> (*Ralph enters as* **Captain**; *Captain as a common sailor. Josephine rushes to his arms.*)

JOSEPHINE:My father —— a common sailor!

CAPT.:.....It is hard, is it not, my dear?

SIR JOSEPH:...This is a very singular **occurrence**; I congratulate you both.(*To Ralph.*) Desire that remarkably fine seaman to step forward.

RALPH:...Corcoran. Three paces to the front—— march!

CAPT.:.....If what?

RALPH:...I don't understand.

CAPT.:.....If you please!

RALPH:...What!

SIR JOSEPH:Perfectly right. If you *please*.

RALPH:...Oh. If you *please*. (*Captain steps forward.*)

SIR JOSEPH...(*to Captain*): You are an extremely fine fellow.

CAPT.:.....Yes, your honour.

SIR JOSEPH:...So it seems that you were Ralph, and Ralph was you.

CAPT.:.....So it seems, your honour.

SIR JOSEPH:...Well, I need not tell you that after this change in your condition, a marriage with your daughter will be out of the question.

CAPT.:.....Don't say that, your honour—— love levels all ranks.

SIR JOSEPH:.:.It does to a considerable extent, but it does not level them as much as that.

SIR JOSEPH...(*handing Josephine to Ralph*): Here —— take her, sir, and mind you treat her kindly.

RALPH and JOSEPHINE:..Oh bliss, oh rapture!

CAPT. and BUT.:.. Oh rapture, oh bliss!

SIR JOSEPH:...Sad my lot and sorry, what shall I do? I cannot live alone!

HEBE:....Fear nothing—— while I live I'll not desert you. I'll soothe and comfort your declining days.

SIR JOSEPH:...No, don't do that.

HEBE:....Yes, but indeed I'd rather——

SIR JOSEPH...(*resigned*): Oh! very well, then!
   Tomorrow morn our vows shall all be plighted,
   Three loving pairs on the same day united!

No. 21 Finale
"Oh joy, oh rapture unforeseen!"

orb of love, Has hung his en-sign high a-bove; The sky is all a-

orb of love, Has hung his en-sign high a-bove; The sky is all a-

orb of love, Has hung his en-sign high a-bove; The sky is all a-

orb of love, Has hung his en-sign high a-bove; The sky is all a-

blaze. We'll chase the lag-ging

blaze. They'll chase the lag-ging

blaze. With woo-ing words and lov-ing song We'll chase the lag-ging

blaze. With woo-ing words They'll chase the lag-ging hours a-hours a-long, And if he finds the maid-en coy, We'll mur-mur forth de-

hours a-lohg, And if he finds the maid-en coy, They'll mur-mur forth de-

hours a-long, And if I find the maid-en coy, We'll mur-mur forth de-

long, And if he finds the maid-en coy, They'll mur-mur forth de-

co-rous joy, In dream - - - y roun-de-

co-rous joy, In dream - - - y roun-de-

co-rous joy, In dream - - - y roun-de-

co-rous joy, In dream-y roun-de-lays, in roun-de-

TENORS

give three cheers, and one cheer more, For the form-er cap-tain of the

BASSES

give three cheers, and one cheer more, For the form-er cap-tain of the

Pin - a - fore, Then give three cheers, and one cheer more, For the

Pin - a - fore, Then give three cheers, and one cheer more, For the

cap-tain of the Pin - a - fore.

BUTTERCUP

For he

cap-tain of the Pin - a - fore.

loves lit-tle But-ter-cup, dear lit-tle But-ter-cup, Though I could nev-er tell

COUSIN HEBE

reck-on up by doz-ens, and your aunts! _____ For he is an

reck-on up by doz-ens, and your aunts! _____ For he is an

Eng-lish-man! _ For _ he him-self has said it,

Eng-lish-man! _ For he him-self has said it,

And it's   That he

And it's great-ly to his cred-it, That he

And it's great-ly to his cred-it, That he

is an Eng - lish - man!___ That he is___ an___

Eng - - - lish - man!

Eng - - - lish - man!

(CURTAIN)